PALMYRA 1885

PALMYRA 1885

The Wolfe Expedition and the Photographs of John Henry Haynes

Benjamin Anderson & Robert G. Ousterhout

'After the bare mountainous desert,
we come gradually on a scene of enchantment,
and though we have come expressly to see the scene,
it breaks upon us as a surprise.'

William Wright, upon arriving at Palmyra, 1895

CORNUCOPIA BOOKS

Cover
Palmyra's Great Colonnade and the hilltop medieval castle of Qalaat Shirkuh (plate 13)

Frontispiece
The Monumental Arch, constructed across the Great Colonnade during the reign of the Roman emperor Septimius Severus (193–211), when Palmyra was at its most prosperous (plate 54)

CONTENTS

PREVIOUS PAGES *Palmyra appears as a forest of columns in this photograph of the ancient city's main street, the Great Colonnade (plate 23)*

INTRODUCTION

'We pitched our tent by the little sun temple,' wrote John Henry Haynes as his party arrived at Palmyra in April 1885, 'setting our table within its sacred precincts.' Nearing the end of their journey, Haynes and his companions had spent the previous months traversing Mesopotamia, looking for a suitable site for an American excavation. They had bid farewell to the Euphrates six days earlier at Deir ez-Zor, following the Roman caravan route across the Syrian Desert. This they confirmed a few hours west of Arak, ancient Aracha, where they noted a Roman milestone – the eighth on Diocletian's Road, the Strata Diocletiana. Palmyra constituted a detour for their party – and was even the cause of some grumbling by its leader, the Rev. William Hays Ward. Although blessed with legendary status and ruins of mythical proportions, Palmyra was not related to their Babylonian investigations at all. Be that as it may, Haynes had been requested by the President of the Archaeological Institute of America to photograph the caravan city as extensively as he could.

The party spent five days at the site: Haynes's journal records their stay as April 11 to 16, although Ward's diary says April 17 to 22 – somewhere in the mudflats of Mesopotamia one or the other had lost track of the days. While his travelling companions recorded inscriptions, Haynes was able to take nearly a hundred photographs – their number limited by the shortness of their visit, the number of glass plates their pack animals could carry, and the technical difficulties of early photography. On his best days, Haynes was able to shoot at most two dozen photographs. Many are stunning views, for Palmyra was and remains a uniquely picturesque city.

For Haynes and the others Palmyra's majestic colonnades and temples offered a dramatic visual contrast to the mud-brick ruins of Babylonia. And although Haynes's photographs are not the earliest views of Palmyra – which had long fascinated adventurers – they constitute one of the most comprehensive early collections of images of the site.

In 2015 the forces of the self-styled Islamic State wantonly destroyed Palmyra's greatest landmarks: the great Temple of Bel (also known as the Temple of Baal), the smaller Temple of Baalshamin, the Monumental Arch, the most visible of the tower tombs and much of the figural sculpture. With recent events having taken such a devastating toll on the monuments, Haynes's photographs are all the more precious.

1 *The second-century Temple of Baalshamin, Palmyra, 1885. Haynes and his companions have left their packs on the brackets of the façade columns of 'the little sun temple', as Haynes called it in his dairy, while they set up camp nearby. The same brackets were used to support the explosives with which the Islamic State blew up the temple 130 years later, in August 2015*

THE PHOTOGRAPHER

John Henry Haynes (1849–1910) may be regarded as the father of American archaeological photography, although he was unrecognised during his lifetime. The majority of his work was published anonymously or credited to others, or it simply remained unpublished – the photographs from the Kroch Library at Cornell University, for example, were almost entirely unpublished and until recently were credited to Haynes's travel companion, John Robert Sitlington Sterrett.

A farm boy from Rowe, Massachusetts, Haynes (known to family and friends as Henry) graduated from Williams College and subsequently joined the first American archaeological expedition to the eastern Mediterranean, in 1880, funded by the newly founded Archaeological Institute of America. Their goal was Knossos, but when the permit to excavate in Crete was denied by the Ottoman government, Haynes found himself in Athens. There he learned photography, working as assistant to William James Stillman, the erstwhile director of the failed Cretan mission, while the latter prepared his second Acropolis folio. His first folio had appeared in 1870 and was a singular achievement. Stillman, sometimes known as 'the American Pre-Raphaelite', was a colourful character and a protégé of John Ruskin, whose picturesque aesthetics formed the underpinnings of his photography.

Incredibly, in less than three months of apprenticeship, while Haynes learned the complex technical details of photography, he unwittingly adopted a Ruskinian picturesque approach to his art. As he framed the view, for example, he would often find a high vantage point, pulling away from the subject to situate it in space. Frequently he utilised rough zigzags in the landscape to lead the eye into space, with significant objects set in the near and middle ground as well as in the distance. Haynes similarly favoured dramatic contrasts of solids and voids, darks and lights. Much of the picturesque aesthetic evident in his photographs derived from landscape painting. His mentor Stillman had applied it to dramatic effect in his photography of the Acropolis. In contrast, Haynes effectively took the Ruskinian picturesque on the road and into the trenches. In doing so, he has left us hundreds of compelling views of the antiquities of Anatolia and the Middle East.

From Athens, Haynes was subsequently dispatched to Assos in northwest Anatolia to become the photographer for the first American Classical excavation, in 1881–83. After that time, Haynes travelled with a camera, documenting his journeys through Anatolia, with major excursions in 1884 and 1887. Rather than return home, Haynes taught at Robert College in Constantinople and later at the American mission school in Aintab (Gaziantep). He joined the Wolfe Expedition to Babylonia of 1884–85, from which his photographs of Palmyra come. The expedition took Haynes out of the familiar Classical world into uncharted territory. Mesopotamia contained strange ancient civilisations with eroded mud-brick architecture and barely understood languages and literatures. But Mesopotamia was Haynes's destiny – or, as some might argue, his fate.

The University of Pennsylvania's excavations at Nippur were the first major result of the explorations of the Wolfe Expedition, for which Haynes was hired as field manager. As a part of American strategy in the region, he also became the first American consul in Baghdad in 1888. Nippur, in the swamps of southern Iraq, was

2 *John Henry Haynes, photographer and archaeologist, in his early fifties. This studio portrait was taken c.1900, after his return from Mesopotamia*

3 *Haynes and Sterrett's party setting off, somewhere in Anatolia, 1884. During the 1880s Haynes travelled several times with the noted epigraphist John Robert Sitlington Sterrett, who appears in white with a pith helmet, bringing up the rear of the caravan. Travel in Anatolia and the Near East was complicated in the 1880s; carrying photographic equipment and delicate glass-plate negatives only added to the complexity*

difficult of access, inhospitable in climate, surrounded by warring tribes, and not particularly attractive. Yet the site offered tantalising clues to the early history of civilisation, and the Babylonian Exploration Fund (BEF) of the University of Pennsylvania was lured by the prospect of a library of cuneiform tablets.

The first expedition (1888–89), led by John Punnett Peters (1852–1921), found barely enough to justify continuing; the season was marred by infighting among the participants, their difficulties exacerbated by the animosity of the locals, who robbed them and burned their camp as they departed, which culminated in mass resignations. The University of Pennsylvania's Assyriologist Hermann Vollrath Hilprecht (1859–1925) simply refused to go back to the site. Only Peters and Haynes returned, reluctantly, for a second, more successful season (1889–90), which found 8,000 tablets, but the conditions were too much for Peters. The stolid Haynes returned alone for a long third campaign (1893–96), during which local conditions deteriorated into what he termed 'Robberdom and Murderland'. Haynes constantly feared for his life but found little sympathy from Peters in Philadelphia, who criticised his insufficient excavation reports and instructed him that 'the Committee wants tablets'.

During the summer of 1894 in Baghdad, Haynes met by chance a travelling MIT architecture graduate, Joseph A. Meyer (1856–94), whom he induced to join the expedition. Meyer's insight and graphic skills made significant contributions to clarifying the architecture at Nippur. More importantly, he provided Haynes with companionship in his 'lonely and desolate life', as the latter wrote in his unpublished account of the Nippur excavation. Less than six months later, however, Meyer was dead from typhoid, and Haynes's mental condition deteriorated. By the time assistance finally arrived in the spring of 1896, Haynes was convinced of imminent danger and insisted on immediate evacuation.

Haynes returned for the fourth and final season (1898–1900), but during his rest and recuperation in the US, to everyone's surprise, he got married. Taciturn and close to fifty, he met the ebullient Cassandria Artella Smith during a visit to the Smithsonian, and married her shortly thereafter. To the consternation of the BEF, he insisted she accompany him to Nippur. While Haynes was no great catch, his family regarded Cassandria as a floozy and a gold-digger. Their relationship quickly deteriorated during the long months at Nippur, and they soon separated. Adding to the tensions, Haynes's assistants Clarence Fisher and Valentine Gere arrived more than eight months late, due to Gere's illness (laid low in Baghdad with 'pleur-pneumonia') and Fisher's indecisiveness (he tended the invalid Gere, then retreated to London, then returned to accompany Gere to Nippur). To complicate matters, Fisher had developed a hopeless, unrequited infatuation with Gere. The atmosphere at the dig house began to resemble an Edward Albee play.

In his memoirs, Gere portrays Haynes as an incompetent bungler, but during the final season in 1900, Haynes hit the mother lode: what was alleged to be the Temple Library, from which 23,000 tablets were extracted. When he heard the news, Hilprecht returned immediately to Nippur for the first time in eleven years and took charge. By that time most of the work was finished, and the tablets had been crated for shipment. Over the course of the next years, however, as scientific director of the expedition, Hilprecht discredited Haynes's accomplishments and claimed responsibility for his discoveries. Haynes vanished from the public eye, succumbing to tuberculosis in 1910.

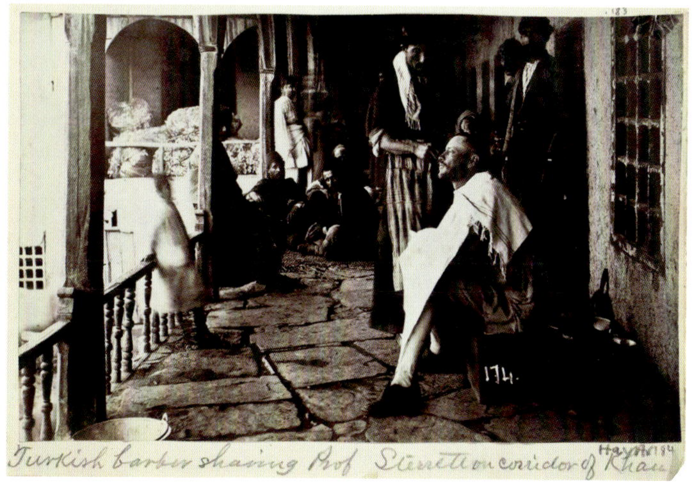

4 *A Turkish barber shaves Sterrett in a 'han' in the central Anatolian town of Malatya as local men look on, 1884*

5 *The Tigris at Baghdad, with the characteristic round, pitch-covered boats known as 'kufa' in the foreground and the pontoon bridge in the distance. Haynes first visited Baghdad with the Wolfe Expedition in 1885, when this view was taken. He was named the first American consul in Baghdad in 1888*

THE WOLFE EXPEDITION

The nineteenth-century fascination with Mesopotamia requires some explanation: why did the archaeologists of the University of Pennsylvania end up in the barren mudflats of southern Mesopotamia instead of somewhere more visually compelling, such as Palmyra? Interest in the ancient Babylonian civilisations had been inspired in part by explorations of British and European adventurer-scholars, the decipherment of cuneiform scripts, and – particularly in America – an abiding familiarity with the Bible.

The foundation of learned societies in America reflects these interests: the oldest specialised organisation was the American Oriental Society, founded in 1842; the Society for Biblical Exegesis and Archaeology followed in 1880. Both had strong interests in the ancient cultures of Mesopotamia. Sir Austen Henry Layard's travels and explorations in the 1840s and 50s had resulted in the publication of his popular romantic travelogues, as well as illustrated excavation reports from his explorations at Nimrud and Nineveh. Many had become enthralled with the literate ancient cultures of the region, whose rich body of literature was known from the cuneiform scripts only recently translated. Many episodes in Mesopotamian mythology seemed to parallel Old Testament events, including the shared tradition of a great flood. Scientific exploration of the region, it was thought, might thus support the veracity of the Bible.

By 1880, Americans had been bitten by the 'Biblical archaeology' bug and thought it expedient to catch up with their European colleagues, both as part of the 'scramble for the past' to fill their new museums, and as part of a civilising mission to ground their emerging nation in world history. Without the resources and tradition of exploration, however, this seemed a difficult challenge. The possibility of an expedition to Babylonia was hotly discussed among the leaders of the American Oriental Society and the Society for Biblical Exegesis and Archaeology. They calculated that an expedition of six months could be supported by a budget of $5,000, and had scarcely begun to solicit funds for the enterprise in 1884 when Mrs Catherine Lorillard Wolfe (1828–87) stepped forward to provide the full amount. A New York socialite, philanthropist and patron of the arts, Mrs Wolfe is remembered today for her financial and artistic bequests to the Metropolitan Museum of Art in New York, but she too was caught up in the Mesopotamia mania.

The expedition was led by the indefatigable Rev. Dr William Hayes Ward (1835–1916), clergyman, amateur Orientalist, prolific writer, and editor of the weekly New York magazine *The Independent*. One of the great public intellectuals of his age, Ward was born to a Massachusetts clerical family: his father, grandfather and great-grandfather had all been pastors in the Congregational Church. Ward followed in their footsteps; he was ordained in 1859 and married in the same year. He subsequently applied to the American Board of Missions for an overseas posting but was rejected because of his wife's delicate health. Instead he found an appointment with the Congregational Home Missionary Society and spent two years ministering in Oskaloosa, Kansas. Ward taught briefly before joining the editorial staff of *The Independent* in 1868, where he spent the rest of his career, rising through the ranks to editor-in-chief, a position he held from 1896 until 1913, the year before his retirement. While remaining active in church and missionary

6 *Somewhere in Mesopotamia, before Haynes and his travelling companions arrived at Palmyra. The vast, empty landscapes could not compete with the visual extravagance Haynes would discover at Palmyra, and his first visit to the region did not inspire picturesque photographs*

7 *Borsippa (Birs Nimrud), an ancient Sumerian city close to Babylon in central Iraq, excavated by Henry Creswicke Rawlinson in 1854 and again by Hormuzd Rassam for the British Museum from 1879 to 1881. The ziggurat, with its distinctive tower, was identified in Talmudic and Arab sources as the Tower of Babel. The Wolfe Expedition visited the site in 1885*

projects throughout his life, Ward was also a fierce abolitionist, a champion of poets, an energetic correspondent and an impressive amateur Orientalist. He was twice president of the American Oriental Society, continuing on his own the study of the Old and New Testaments, as well as Semitic languages and Near Eastern archaeology, and developing a particular fascination with the cylinder seals of Assyria and Babylonia. An ardent advocate for Babylonian archaeology, he seemed the logical person to direct the expedition.

Ward was joined by the classicist and epigraphist John Robert Sitlington Sterrett (1851–1914). Sterrett had received his PhD from the University of Munich in 1880 and was in residence at the newly formed American School of Classical Studies at Athens when he was approached to join the Wolfe Expedition. A disciple of Sir William Ramsay, the distinguished scholar and specialist in the historical geography of Asia Minor, with whom he had travelled, Sterrett was devoted to recording the Greek inscriptions of Anatolia as part of a larger interest in historical geography, and he corresponded with the German geographer and map-maker Heinrich Kiepert. Sterrett subsequently taught at several American institutions before becoming Professor of Greek at Cornell University in 1901. His fascination with ancient Anatolia persisted despite his new responsibilities, and in 1907–08 he sent a team of former students on the Cornell Expedition to Asia Minor and the Assyro-Babylonian Orient.

As the Wolfe Expedition came together, John Henry Haynes was working as a tutor at Robert College, Istanbul. Invited to join as field manager and photographer, he jumped at the opportunity for further exploration, resigning his position to do so. Limited in his travels by his own lack of funds, and earning a 'missionary's wage' as a tutor, he depended on the financial support of others – even the camera he used was not his own but belonged to the Archaeological Institute of America. Haynes and Sterrett were friends, having collaborated at the Assos excavations in 1883, and the two had travelled across Anatolia together in the summer of 1884, with Haynes photographing antiquities as Sterrett recorded inscriptions and milestones. Both were considerably more familiar with travel in the Orient than was Ward, and both spoke serviceable Turkish. The younger and better travelled men would occasionally clash with the more eminent Ward, who was firm but often erratic in his opinions and expectations. 'He little knows his own mind in anything,' writes Haynes dismissively, adding, 'He must have a sister that possesses a well balanced mind that advises and controls him perhaps without his conscious knowledge but who nevertheless tempers and tones everything he does.'

A nineteen-year-old Armenian, Daniel Z. Noorian (1865–1929), completed the team as its translator. Although unnamed in the official accounts of the Wolfe Expedition – he is referred to simply as 'an intelligent Armenian' – he appears regularly in Ward's and Haynes's diaries. After the conclusion of the expedition, in fact, Ward brought Noorian to the United States, where he resided with Ward's family in Newark and attended school. In 1888 he returned to the eastern Mediterranean to join the University of Pennsylvania's expedition to Nippur – along with Haynes. Already in 1885 Noorian was engaged in buying and selling antiquities, and he subsequently became a successful importer, dealing in 'rare and beautiful objects of artistic and archaeological value', as his letterhead declared. With a showroom in Manhattan, he channelled artworks and antiquities to many major European and American museums.

After discussing their plans with Osman Hamdi Bey, director of the Imperial Museum in Constantinople, the party sailed to Mersin by way of Smyrna, where Sterrett met them, at the end of October 1884. From Mersin they travelled eastward along the Mediterranean coast before heading inland to the Fertile Crescent, often enjoying the hospitality of American missions along the way. As a Congregational minister, Ward was always on the lookout for Protestant Christians. At the Mardin mission, they signed the guestbook, identifying themselves as 'the Wolfe gang'. In December they visited Mosul and Erbil and found the latter particularly impressive. However, Sterrett fell gravely ill at Erbil, and the expedition pushed on to Baghdad, where he was placed under the care of the British consul. The others continued without him,

8 *Nippur in southern Iraq, where Haynes excavated from 1889 to 1900, showing the temple courtyard in the process of excavation. Haynes eventually found beauty in the Mesopotamian landscape, here capturing c.1894 an atmospheric image of contrasting dark and light; workers appear like a train of ants against the massive architecture and the vast empty landscape*

taking note of the great mounds, remnants of ancient cities, palaces and temples. South of Babylon they entered areas no American had previously traversed, and no European for several decades.

The purpose of the explorations was to find a suitable site for an American excavation in Babylonia. In southern Mesopotamia they visited Nuffar, ancient Nippur, a Sumerian city dedicated to the god Enlil. This was one of the sites Osman Hamdi Bey had encouraged them to consider, and Ward noted the presence of the Marsh Arabs nearby, who could be hired as workers. As they headed northward again, Sterrett had recovered enough to join them for the return journey through the Syrian Desert. In the spring of 1885 they made the month-long desert crossing by way of Dura-Europos and Palmyra. At Dura, which Haynes recorded simply as a 'Sassanian city', he photographed the impressive Palmyrene Gate *(plate 9)*. (Accounts of the site customarily attribute its first archaeological documentation to Friedrich Sarre, who visited in 1898.)

As noted, Haynes had been requested to photograph Palmyra by the Archaeological Institute of America. According to Haynes, the Orientalist Ward 'cared nothing for Palmyra before coming' but 'was delighted with the ample ruins here'. Accordingly, they extended their stay, and Haynes was able to take almost a hundred photographs. Afterwards the expedition continued to Homs, Damascus and finally Beirut, where they effectively ended their explorations in April 1885. Ward returned to New York, taking Noorian with him, and Haynes to Constantinople, before assuming a new post in Aintab. In Beirut, Sterrett received news that Mrs Wolfe had supplied funds for further travel, and in May he set off on yet another epigraphic survey of central Anatolia.

Ward's account of the expedition was published in 1886, advocating further American exploration and excavation in Mesopotamia. The team had identified several potential excavation sites, including Anbar in the north and Nuffar (Nippur) in the south. Facing more restrictive legislation by the Ottoman government concerning archaeology, however, he considered surveying and mapping without a permit as a viable alternative, noting that it would always be possible to purchase antiquities in the bazaar. Led by the University of Pennsylvania, the Americans undertook the excavation of Nippur in 1889, with Haynes and Noorian as members of the team. They did not return to Palmyra.

9 The Palmyrene Gate, principal entrance to the caravan city of Dura-Europos on the Euphrates, photographed by Haynes in 1885. It faces towards Palmyra, the next major city, six days' travel across the Syrian Desert to the west. Only officially discovered in 1898, Dura-Europos preserves significant remains from Late Antiquity, having been abandoned after the Sassanian siege of AD 256. This may be the first photograph of the site ever taken

Following pages

10 *A panorama of the ruins of Palmyra at dawn. Haynes would take nearly a hundred glass-plate photographs of the caravan city in the Syrian Desert in just five days in April 1885. This view is taken from the medieval castle of Qalaat Shirkuh, looking east towards the Temple of Bel, with the Great Colonnade in front of it and the oasis behind. Haynes often sought high vantage points, pulling away from his subject to situate it dramatically in space*

PALMYRA AND ITS DESERT QUEEN

As an oasis in the middle of the Syrian Desert, the site of Palmyra has been occupied for millennia. In the Assyrian archives, as in modern Arabic, it is known as Tadmur; and a city of the same name appears in the Hebrew Bible (2 *Chronicles* 8:4) as a foundation of King Solomon. The area was blessed with underground springs that gush forth from the mountains to the north and west, which rendered it a welcome stopping point for caravans passing between the Euphrates and the Mediterranean – the Efqa Spring beneath the hill of Jebel Muntar is particularly significant and was the site of cultic activity from an early period. During the civil wars at the end of the Roman Republic, Marc Antony sent an armed expedition against Palmyra, 'bringing the trifling accusation against its inhabitants, that being on the frontier between the Romans and the Parthians, they had avoided taking sides between them; for being merchants, they bring the products of India and Arabia from Persia and dispose of them in the Roman territory; but in fact, Antony's intention was to enrich his horsemen' (Appian, *The Civil Wars*, V.1.9).

The oldest preserved Palmyrene inscription, characteristically composed in both Greek and the local dialect of Aramaic, dates to AD 19; it records the contribution of a local worthy to the construction of the Temple of Bel. By the mid-first century Palmyra was increasingly absorbed within the Roman sphere of influence. Latin began to appear alongside Greek and Aramaic in the local funerary epitaphs, and at least one Palmyrene served as an envoy between Rome and the Persian courts to the east. Pliny wrote that the city, 'placed between the two great empires of Rome and Parthia, still maintains its independence; never failing, at the very first moment that a rupture between them is threatened, to attract the careful attention of both'. And indeed Palmyra did sustain a kind of autonomy, both culturally and politically, even as it officially became part of the province of Syria. Above all, trade flourished. The Palmyrene Tariff, inscribed on a stone plaque in AD 137 and displayed outside the Senate building, prescribes duties on goods that pass through the city and its territories (slaves, purple-dyed wool, perfumed oils, salted fish, livestock) and on those exchanged within the town (garments, pine nuts, camels, bronze statues and the services of prostitutes).

In the second century Palmyra was at its height economically, rivalling Antioch in importance. The Tariff proudly names the city 'Hadriana Palmyra' in honour of the emperor Hadrian, who had visited in AD 129. Much of the monumental construction dates to this period and is increasingly Roman in character: the Theatre, the expanding Agora and the Great Colonnade that still dominates the ancient city's image. At the same time the local worthies ceased construction of the characteristic tower tombs that had served as family mausolea for the past two centuries, turning instead to underground chambers and above-ground 'temple tombs' that more closely resembled funerary complexes in other cities of the empire. Despite the disruption to trade caused by the Roman-Parthian war of AD 162–165, ambitious construction continued through the second half of the second century, including the Monumental Arch and tetrapylon that punctuated the Great Colonnade.

The late second and early third centuries were marked by renewed war between Rome and Persia; although trade may have decreased, Palmyra's ties to the capital grew stronger. Under the Severan dynasty the city became a *colonia*, an honorific status granted directly by the emperor; and its residents erected portraits of the imperial family at the entrance to the Agora. Many Palmyrenes adopted Roman names, such as Julius Aurelius Marona, whose house-tomb stands to the north of the city *(plate 40)*. Palmyra even hosted the emperor Severus Alexander (reg. 222–35), the second imperial visit in as many centuries.

Severus was the last of his dynasty, and his assassination plunged the empire into a prolonged crisis. In Persia, meanwhile, Parthian rule had collapsed and been replaced by the shahs of the Sassanian dynasty, whose territorial ambitions posed a new threat to Rome. In 260 the emperor Valerian was captured by the Sassanians. This humiliation marked a nadir of Roman imperial power; a fourth-century historian recalled that the shah used the captive emperor as a footstool when mounting his carriage, proclaiming 'that this was how things truly were, not as Romans painted them in pictures'. In the resulting power vacuum Palmyra rapidly rose to global prominence. A local worthy named Odenathus led the defence against the Persians, campaigning throughout the 260s in Syria and Mesopotamia. The emperor Gallienus, son of Valerian, was preoccupied with invasions and revolts in Europe, and granted Odenathus the title of *corrector totius orientis*, 'corrector of the whole east'. After Odenathus was assassinated in 267, his widow Zenobia claimed for her eight-year-old son Vaballathus the far more ambitious title of 'king of kings'.

11 *Zenobia 'Augusta', Queen of Palmyra*

Under Zenobia, the Palmyrenes moved decisively from maintenance of order to fully fledged revolt against Rome. The city's troops marched south and east through Arabia and Egypt, and north and west through Antioch and into central Anatolia, eventually controlling much of the eastern portion of the Roman Empire. Coins struck in Antioch declared Zenobia 'Augusta', her son 'Imperator Caesar Augustus'. The emperor Aurelian could no longer ignore such pretensions; in 272 he led a great army eastward to restore Roman authority. Palmyra was sacked in the following year, and the 'Warrior Queen' Zenobia was taken captive and brought back to Rome.

If much about these events remains obscure, a romantic legend quickly grew up around Zenobia, the Queen of the Desert, who defied a mighty empire. Already in the fourth century Roman historians remembered her as the woman who knew how to rule in an age of incompetent men. One imagined a dialogue between Aurelian and the captive queen, who declares: 'You are an emperor indeed, for you win victories, but Gallienus and the others I never regarded as emperors. Believing Victory to be a woman like me, I desired to become a partner in the royal power.' The same historian recalls a triumph in which Zenobia was paraded through the streets of Rome 'decked with jewels and in golden chains' – whose weight, however, was 'borne by others'. Far from being humiliated, Zenobia was said to have retired to an estate near Hadrian's palace at Tivoli, 'where she lived with her children in the manner of a Roman matron'. Her memory continued to inspire later writers and artists as diverse as Chaucer and Tiepolo, and she was the subject of at least eight operas. Despite her brief rule, Palmyra is remembered today as the city of Zenobia.

The Roman historians remember the queen's public persona as hybrid: 'It was rather in the manner of the Persians that she received worship and in the manner of the Persian kings that she banqueted; but it was in the manner of a Roman emperor that she came forth to public assemblies.' A similar impression is made by the multitude of surviving Palmyrene funerary portraits, in which the local notables stare forth at us with startlingly proud and direct gazes *(plate 12)*.

In costume and gesture they display a mixture of East and West, local and cosmopolitan. Women are often richly garbed, with headdresses or headbands of a local type combined with characteristically Roman veils. Their gestures usually follow Roman conventions: women raise their hands to their chins or finger their veils in a typical sign of *pudicitia* – modesty or virtue *(plate 49)*. Others, however, may raise a hand with the palm facing outwards – a gesture regarded as apotropaic in Semitic culture *(plate 50)*. Men wear a combination of chiton and himation, with the right arm extended from the sling in the drapery, following Roman custom. Full-length figures, however, wear characteristically Eastern pantaloons, but they are often represented reclining on ornamented couches, banqueting in the Roman manner. Sometimes attributes will indicate profession: for example, a scroll held by a figure may mark him as a businessman or scribe. Priests are easily identified by their Eastern headgear, a tall cylindrical hat known as a modius. They usually wear a chlamys attached on the shoulder with a brooch, and they hold vessels associated with their sacerdotal activities. Gestures between individuals also signal family ties, as they do in Roman Republican portraiture. Taken together, the many surviving Palmyrene portraits provide a sense of the complexities of identity construction in a colonial context, drawing on both Roman conventions and local customs to express elite social status or a more specific individuality.

After the Roman reconquest, Palmyra's position was increasingly defined by its military significance, as a link in a chain of outposts fortified against the Sassanians, and less by trade. The city was expanded to the northwest under Diocletian (reg. 284–305) to lodge the Roman legion, and was surrounded by a new circuit wall at the same time. With the imperial embrace of Christianity in the fourth century, Palmyra followed suit. Already in 325, a Bishop of Palmyra attended the Council of Nicaea, and churches dominate the new monumental constructions of these centuries. A new episcopal quarter, composed of four churches and a bishop's palace, grew up to the north of the Great Colonnade.

In the sixth century, Procopius, court historian to the emperor Justinian, described Palmyra as a lonely outpost, 'built in a neighbourless region by men of former times', and newly fortified against 'the raids of the Saracens'. The Syrian historian Malalas, writing around the same time, relates some of the stories of the deep antiquity of the desert city: it was here that David had slain Goliath, and here that Nebuchadnezzar had sacked a garrison of Jewish soldiers on his way to Jerusalem. The legends were sustained by the monumental remains of the city's heyday: al-Nabigha al-Dhubyani, greatest of the pre-Islamic poets writing in Arabic, recalled that God had commanded Solomon to 'subject the jinn! as I ordered them to build Tadmur with bricks and marble'.

With the rise of Islam and the Arab conquest of Syria in the 630s, Palmyra became part of the new world empire. The city's remains continued to inspire poets, in particular a statue of two women (presumably one of the funerary monuments) who became a favourite trope for persistence against the passage of time:

> *O maidens of the people of Tadmur,*
> *Do you not tire from long waiting?*
> *For you do not rest on soft cushions,*
> *But on a hard block of stone.*

In the 740s the Palmyrenes supported a revolt against the ruling caliph, Marwan II, who pulled down parts of the city's walls in retribution, giving rise to further stories of the funerary monuments that emerged in the process.

Palmyra in the first Islamic century was a bustling city. The churches continued in use and bishops continued to be ordained, even as a mosque was constructed at the centre of the Roman city, between the tetrapylon and the Theatre. A new market consisting of some fifty shops was constructed along the Great Colonnade, suggesting a resurgence of trade. With the end of the Umayyad dynasty, however, and the construction of the new capital city of Baghdad, Palmyra became a provincial town, if still a regular stop for those crossing the desert. In the twelfth century it hosted the traveller Benjamin of Tudela, who recalled its construction by Solomon and noted the presence of a Jewish community with three rabbis; in the fourteenth century Ibn Battuta passed through and took the opportunity to quote al-Nabigha's verses.

In these years the modest population began to cluster within the temenos (enclosure) of the Temple of Bel, where Arabic inscriptions testify to successive campaigns of fortification and repair in the twelfth and thirteenth centuries. A fifteenth-century edict, also posted within the temenos, confirmed the residents' grazing rights on the surrounding mountains. The major new construction of the period was Qalaat Shirkuh *(plate 85)*, the impressive fortification on top of the hill to the northwest of the site that stands in the background, framed by the Great Colonnade, on the cover of this volume.

12 *Startlingly direct in their gaze, the funerary portraits from the collection of the 'mudir' (governor) depict the elite of ancient Palmyra in a fashionable mix of Roman and Palmyrene dress: a man wears a chiton and himation, with one arm extended from the sling of drapery and the other clutching a scroll; a bejewelled woman wears a Palmyrene headdress with a Roman veil; a bearded man reclines at a funerary banquet, wearing typically Eastern pantaloons*

13 *Palmyra's Great Colonnade frames the façade of the Temple Tomb. On the distant hilltop is the medieval castle of Qalaat Shirkuh. On the right are the ruins of the domestic quarter*

THE TOPOGRAPHY OF PALMYRA

Covering an immense area of more that ten square kilometres, the remains of the city form a rough oval, with the Temple of Bel at the southeast end and the Camp of Diocletian at the northwest. The major religious centre of the city, the Temple of Bel was enclosed within a massive, solid masonry temenos, or perimeter wall, measuring c. 205 by 210 metres, entered from the west through a propylaeum 35 metres wide. Inside, the temenos was lined with porticoes on all sides, with double porticoes at north, east and south. Altars for blood sacrifice stood in front of the temple proper, raised on a platform above the temenos pavement. The entryway, positioned off-axis on the long western side, led through a prostyle colonnade and into the *cella* (inner chamber), whose two sanctuaries (or *adytons*) were set at the north and south ends, respectively.

The spine of the city was the Great Colonnade, the equivalent of a Roman decumanus, which stretches an extraordinary 1,100 metres in length, running west to east and connecting temple to camp. The Colonnade is composed of three primary segments of unequal length and divergent orientation. The shortest stretch leads from the Temple to the Monumental Arch, which was cleverly designed to conceal the westward bend in the street. The adjoining segment leads through the monumental heart of the Roman city, passing the Theatre and Agora to the south and the baths to the north, before terminating in a second transitional element, a tetrapylon set within an oval plaza. From here the Great Colonnade follows a more northerly course for its third and longest section, passing through the residential blocks, some of which still preserve the remains of fine peristyle houses. The northwest terminus of the Colonnade is marked by a second-century funerary temple. At this point a second, much shorter, colonnaded street runs to the south, passing the gridded military Camp of Diocletian at the east with its apsed *principia (plate 42)* and terminating in a second oval forum before the Damascus Gate.

The colonnaded street was a characteristic feature of Roman urban planning in the East, as well as in North Africa, although Palmyra's porticoes are perhaps the most spectacular ones to be preserved. About half of the estimated 375 columns of the Great Colonnade are still standing, with most just under 10 metres tall. Built in several sections, most of the porticoes date to the prosperous second century, when the brackets of the columns carried statues honouring the local worthies who contributed to the urban construction. Altogether Palmyra appears as a city of colonnades: even minor cross streets were framed with columns *(plates 21–25)*. This impression is augmented by the almost total disintegration of brick walls. Thus many residential and commercial areas of the city preserve their peristyles but not their walls.

The screens of columns are interrupted only by those ashlar walls that framed the most pretentious buildings: the Theatre, Agora and Tariff Court to the south of the Great Colonnade, and especially the Temple of Baalshamin – Haynes's 'little sun temple' – to the north. Constructed in AD 130, immediately following Hadrian's visit, this temple displays a more conventional Roman plan, with an axial, colonnaded façade facing eastward. But it honours the 'Lord of the Heavens', a Semitic weather god. Further sanctuaries established throughout the city honoured regionally significant deities: the Temple of Nabu, set immediately to the southwest of the Monumental Arch, was dedicated to a Mesopotamian god of wisdom, while a temple adjacent to the

Camp of Diocletian was dedicated to the Arabian goddess Allat.

To the west of the living city stretched a city of the dead. The Valley of the Tombs outside the Damascus Gate was lined with towers enclosing multi-storeyed burial chambers, many connected to underground hypogea. A second cluster of tower tombs fronts the northern flanks of the hill known as Umm al-Belqis *(plate 26)*. To the northwest of the city a second hill is crowned by Qalaat Shirkuh, the medieval castle, almost on an axis with the Great Colonnade. Immediately to the south lies the oasis, which has

14 *Seen from above, the grid plan of the city becomes apparent. This is a distant view from the hill of Jebel Muntar (see plate 19), looking northeast towards Diocletian's Camp, with the ruined fortification wall and the remains of the Damascus Gate on the right. The Marona house-tomb (plate 40), built by a wealthy merchant in AD 236, is isolated in the distance*

15 *Another panorama of the city, looking southeast from the Jebel Husseiniye, across Diocletian's Camp. To the left of the honorific column, only the door frame of the Temple of Allat survives (see plate 27)*

springs in its northern part and is separated from the city by the *wadi*.

Because the Wolfe Expedition visited before any modern excavation had taken place, its members saw a very different Palmyra from that visible to the more recent visitor. For example, the Theatre and the oval Forum with its tetrapylon do not appear in Haynes's photos, although once uncovered and restored, they became among the most photographed antiquities of the city. Other monuments were partially buried, like the Temple of Baalshamin and the *principia* (or Temple of the Standards) at Diocletian's Camp, whose foundations were only later exposed. The team also had limited access to the Temple of Bel, which

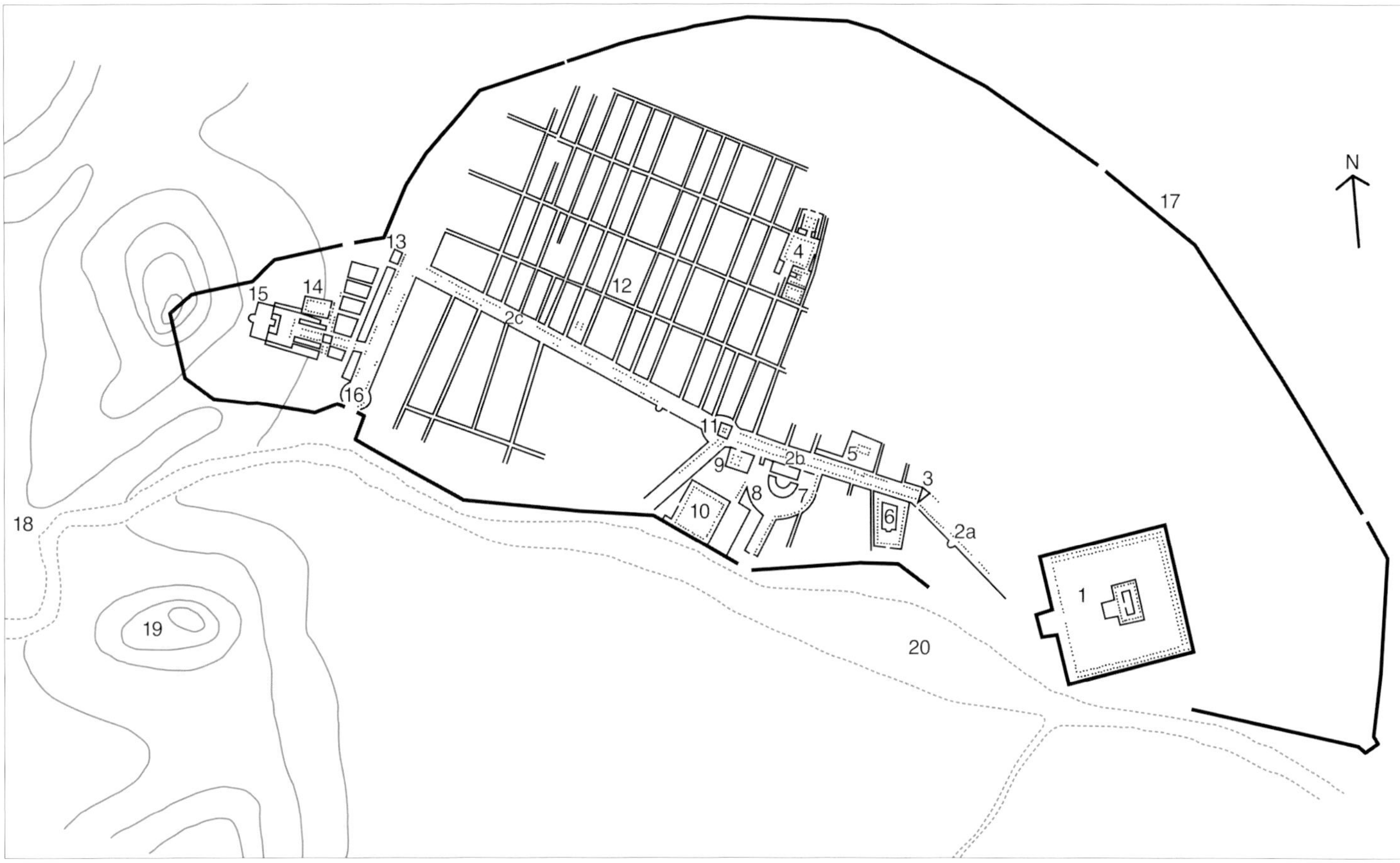

had been completely enveloped by a village of mud brick and rubble. And because the visit to Palmyra was effectively a detour for the Wolfe Expedition, none of the team was fully prepared to understand what they were seeing. 'Not having made any study of Waddington and others,' commented Ward, 'all was new.'

Haynes for his part is annoyingly vague in his records of the photographs taken, with occasional mistakes: for example, identifying the surviving peristyle colonnade of a house as a mausoleum *(plate 70)*. The Temple of Allat is listed in his records simply as 'Doorway and fluted columns' *(plate 27)*; the Temple of Bel as 'Old temple, now used as mosque'.

Plan of Palmyra (B. Anderson)

1. Temple of Bel
2. Great Colonnade
3. Monumental Arch
4. Temple of Baalshamin
5. Baths of Diocletian
6. Temple of Nabu
7. Theatre
8. Tariff Court
9. Umayyad Mosque
10. Agora
11. Tetrapylon
12. Episcopal Quarter
13. Funerary Temple
14. Temple of Allat
15. Camp of Diocletian
16. Damascus Gate
17. Walls of Diocletian
18. Valley of the Tombs
19. Umm al-Belqis
20. Wadi

16 *A view across the southern sector of the city seen from Diocletian's Camp, with the Temple of Bel in the distance. Haynes took the photograph standing on the apse wall of the 'principia', or Temple of the Standards (see plate 42). Emphasising the spatial context, he composed the view with objects of interest in distinct bands: the foreground, the middle distance and the far distance*

17 *A panorama of the city, looking southeast from the Jebel Husseiniye, across Diocletian's Camp, with the fortification wall in the foreground and the Temple of Bel in the distance*

18 *Looking eastward from Umm al-Belqis as the sun sets, with Tower Tomb 71 in the foreground. A rough diagonal line, the ruins of the city's fortification wall, leads the eye towards the Temple of Bel, which appears in the distance, immediately above the tower*

19 *A lone figure rests against a column, looking westward towards the Jebel Muntar and the tower tombs at Umm al-Belqis. Fascinated by the myriad colonnades, Haynes gradually realised he could use them to dramatic effect, framing views of the monuments in the distance*

20 *The great temenos of the Temple of Bel, the walled precinct of the principal religious sanctuary of Palmyra, seen from near the northwest. The final stretch of the Great Colonnade connecting to the temenos may never have been completed. The enclosure is well preserved at its northwest corner, where the outer wall is lined with pilasters. The temple was destroyed in 2015*

21 *A view looking southeast towards the centre of Palmyra. In the middle of the photograph is the Great Colonnade, or decumanus, the spine of the city. To the right is the temenos of the Temple of Bel and on the far right the colonnade of a cross street (see plate 24)*

22 *The eastern segment of the Great Colonnade, with the Temple of Bel in the distance. The distinctive brackets were designed to hold statues*

23 *Looking across the decumanus, overlapping ranges of colonnades create a puzzling perspective: 'Wherever you move, columns without number block your path,' commented William Wright in 1895*

24 *Brackets cast long midday shadows onto the columns along a cross street, while portions of the Great Colonnade and the funerary temple appear in the distance, with the view to the medieval castle blocked by the architrave*

25 *A view looking northeast across the ruins of the city testifies to the column mania of ancient Palmyra. As William Wright noted in 1895, 'Little houses had their tiers of little columns, and great houses had their tiers of correspondingly great columns. Public edifices… had their quota of lofty columns. Little streets and public squares all had their rows of columns…'*

26 *A view from the area of Diocletian's Camp towards Umm al-Belqis, with Tower Tomb 71 on the left and the Tomb of Iamblichus (Yamliku Mokimo, no. 51, dated AD 83) on the right; in between are tombs no. 70 (Julius Aurelius Bolma, last used in 234), no. 68 (Bene Ba'a, AD 83), no. 67 (Hairan Belsuri, AD 33), no. 65 and no. 63 (Banai family, AD 79). Tombs 71, 51 and 63 were destroyed in 2015*

27 *Only the door frame still stands at the Temple of Allat, an Arabian goddess equated with Ishtar. Built in the second century AD, it was subsequently enveloped by the Camp of Diocletian. Sterrett in his pith helmet and a companion pose amid the ruins*

BEASTS, MEN AND STONES

Palmyra in Photography and Imagination

The expedition's relative unfamiliarity with the site was in some senses an advantage. By the nineteenth century the visual representation of Palmyra in European publications had solidified around a set of clichés that emphasised the heroism of the explorer and suppressed the independent perseverance of a local community. Haynes's views, by contrast, give us a relatively innocent view of the site, refreshingly free of the standard tropes.

In October 1691 a small party of Englishmen rode into Tadmur (known to them as Tadmor or Tedmor), reaching their goal after six days' journey from Aleppo. As they crested the stark hill to the northeast of the ancient city, a forest of columns, the ruinous expanse of Roman Palmyra, will have stretched out beneath them. However, when the Rev. William Halifax addressed an account of the party's findings to a learned public, he drew his readers' attention first to the medieval castle at the top of the hill. This was surrounded by a ditch 'not having the least appearance of moisture therein; which made it therefore seem more strange that a Wild Boar should rush out thence amongst our Horses, when we rode up to take a more particular View of the place'.

That swine is but one of the menagerie that crowds the memoirs of the early travellers. In 1678 the merchants Timothy Lanoy and Aaron Goodyear passed through al-Andarin, two days south of Aleppo, where they encountered 'a dozen Buffalo's' that provided a local family with milk and drew their ploughs. The following day brought them to a desert 'troubled with Rat-holes in great numbers, like Coney-boroughs, which by the sinking of the Earth, very much incommoded our Horses and Mules. These Rats have

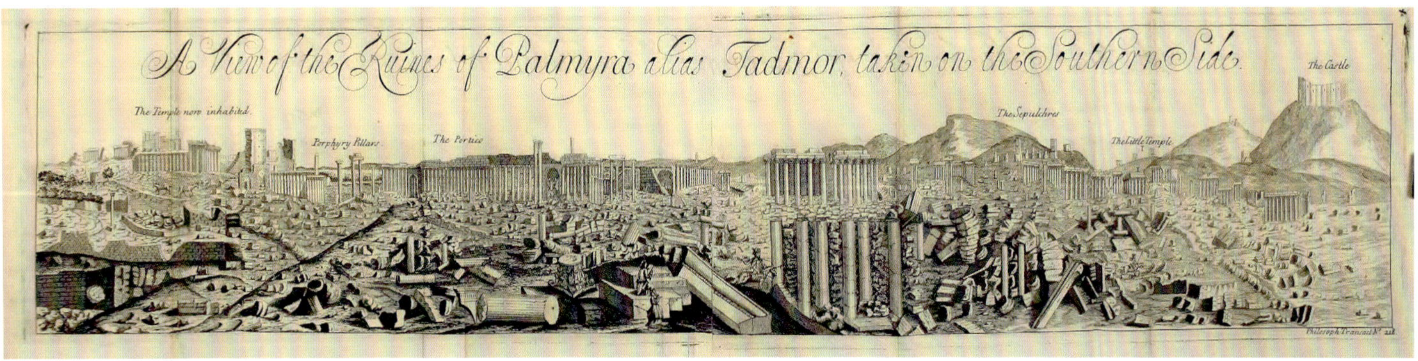

28 *The first widely distributed view of Palmyra, by Lanoy and Goodyear, appeared in 1695 in the Royal Society's 'Philosophical Transactions' (see inside back flap)*

at the ends of their Tails a bush of Hair, and the Arabs eat them all, excepting one part'.

When the merchants' party arrived in Tadmur they were greeted by the local heavy, one Melkam, with a repast of 'Coffee, Camels-Flesh and Dates'. But the parley soured when the host demanded '4000 Dollars as a Present'. The visitors paid as much as they were able, after which 'this Melkam told us, that if we had not submitted our selves to his Demands, he was resolved to Fight us, after this Method: Loading 50 Camels with Baggs of Sand, and making small holes in the Baggs for the Sand to drop out, he would drive these Camels abreast upon us before the Wind, that the Sand might blow in our Eyes, and we spending our Bullets on the Camels, might so be easily overthrown'.

The merchants complained of their mistreatment to the Ottoman governor in Aleppo, and Melkam was executed, thus confirming his earlier apprehension 'that now we knew the way through the Desert, we might inform the Turks to their Ruin and Destruction'. Thirteen years later, when Lanoy and Goodyear returned in the company of the Rev. Halifax (by now Chaplain of Aleppo), they met with no further demands for dollars, but with a still wider assortment of fauna, including 'Gazels', desert serpents and the new hunting hawk who inadvertently assured their positive reception by a local emir ('otherwise he had not been in a good humour all that night, being a Man that delights very much in Sport').

Back in England, these travellers' reports provoked various scholars, among them the astronomer Edmond Halley, to comb ancient literature for references to the desert city. But not until 1751 did an expedition return to examine the physical remains. James Dawkins, whose father owned a sugar plantation in Jamaica, both funded and joined the party that set out from Damascus. Dr Samuel Johnson later remarked: 'The only great instance that I have ever known of the enjoyment of wealth was that of Jamaica Dawkins, who going to visit Palmyra, and hearing that the way was infested by robbers, hired a troop of Turkish horse to guard him.'

We owe a more extensive account of the company to Robert Wood, an accompanying antiquarian and author of the 1753 folio edition that tied his name for ever to Palmyra. The scale of the caravan beggars belief: not only 'Arab horsemen, armed with guns and pikes', but also 'about two hundred persons, and about the same number of beasts for carriage, consisting of an odd mixture of horses, camels, mules and asses'. Wood also mentions, but does not explain, the presence of a number of cattle.

29 *Robert Wood's 'The Ruins of Palmyra, Otherwise Tedmor, in the Desart' was published in 1753. The lavish folio volume literally made its author's name (henceforth he was 'Palmyra Wood') and inspired countless architects with its details of the city's Roman monuments. This view looks east across the temenos court of the Temple of Bel towards the entrance to the temple proper*

If we turn to the first pictures of Palmyra to reach a wide audience, the veritable zoo of the texts is reduced to a spare triad: donkey, horse and camel. The publication of Lanoy and Goodyear's journal in the Royal Society of London's *Philosophical Transactions* was accompanied by a great fold-out panorama labelled *A View of the Ruines of Palmyra alias Tadmor, taken on the Southern Side (plate 28)*: or, as the authors modestly describe it, 'a kind of rude Draught which we had taken of the Place'. The landscape is a tumble of columns and blocks, little peopled. The contemporary settlement within the Temple of Bel is designated by a title ('The Temple now inhabited') but represented only by the donkey and horse that forage outside *(see inside back flap)*.

Wood's far more ambitious volume presents two kinds of image of the ruins, all of them prepared by the expedition's draughtsman, Giovanni Battista Borra. In the measured architectural drawings, presumed lacunae have been restored and all setting removed, while the picturesque views represent (in Wood's words) the 'present state of decay'. The views are peopled exclusively by members of the visiting party: the foreigners, who sketch and discuss, and their guard, 'our Arab horsemen, who engaged in mock fights with each other for our entertainment, and shewed a surprising firmness of seat, and dexterity in the management of their horses'. A view of the interior of the great temple depicts the contemporary dwellings (labelled C on the accompanying legend 'the hutts of the Arabs') as uninhabited; the only figures are at lower right, three lance-bearers who converse amid a jumble of coffers, capitals and columns.

The introduction of the camel, so prominent in the travellers' texts, to the visual repertoire of Palmyreana was left to the Scottish painter Gavin Hamilton. *Wood and Dawkins Discovering Palmyra* (1758) hangs today in Edinburgh, a monumental (or unwieldy) canvas of ten feet by thirteen, but the image found a much wider public through an engraving by John Hall. In the centre the heroes stride forth in toga and boots before a sceptical guardsman; on the left the hindquarters of a fine steed partially occlude the view to the great portico and the Monumental Arch; while above them all a palm trunk brusquely tosses its hair. On the right, finally, a camel and his rider parse a garbled transcription of one of the memorial epigraphs published in Wood's volume. The text is bracketed by consoles that carry a plinth on which a female effigy lies prone.

These early views of Palmyra depict a less inhabited city than the travellers saw, one stripped not only of boar and gazelle, but also of the local human community. Tadmur, in truth, was never abandoned, even if the size of the settlement had contracted steadily from its peak in the second and third centuries AD. Indeed, in his later writings Wood claimed that his knowledge of its 'pristine inhabitants' gave him a special understanding of the poetry of Homer, since 'the Arabs boast a purer and more unmixed antiquity, than any other nation'.

Such ethnographic ruminations were overlooked, however, as Palmyra became a symbol for the transience of earthly power. This image was crystallised in the frontispiece of Constantin de Volney's *Les ruines, ou méditation sur les révolutions des empires* of 1791. In the

30 *The Scottish painter Gavin Hamilton (1723–1798) is best known for his treatment of scenes from ancient literature and history. His rendition of 'Wood and Dawkins Discovering Palmyra' (1758), which hangs today in the Scottish National Gallery, casts the explorers as latter-day Romans. The subject proved popular and was reproduced in multiple printed editions*

foreground a turbaned figure sits on a stone-strewn hill. An owl perches above in a palm tree, while on the left a distinctly French dog looks out across the plain below, which is dominated by the familiar forms of the Temple of Bel, the Monumental Arch and the Great Colonnade. The legend beneath delivers the moral: 'Here once flourished an opulent city; here was the seat of a powerful empire. Yes, a living multitude once animated the walls of these places, now so desolate.'

In the spring of 1785, as Volney awaited passage from Alexandria to Marseilles, he met Louis-François Cassas (1756–1827), an exceptionally talented draughtsman who had already devoted years to the documentation of ruins in Italy and Turkey. Perhaps Volney

31 *Despite its author's noble birth, Constantin de Volney's work on the transience of empires, written in the first years of the French Revolution, was a robustly republican work. Among its admirers was Thomas Jefferson, whose English translation of Volney's book was published anonymously in 1802*

encouraged Cassas to undertake the journey across the desert to Palmyra, where, in the event, he arrived in May of the same year and took up residence in one of the houses within the temple. He stayed for over a month, daily measuring and drawing the ruins.

Cassas's finished views were distributed in a piecemeal and haphazard fashion between 1798 and 1803 as part of an ill-fated venture in publishing, the *Voyage pittoresque de la Syrie*. One plate depicts the artist's arrival much as he described it in his journal: 'I was told that the chief of the Arabs wished to see me; he had already been informed that I bore him some gifts. I found him crouching with various members of his retinue at the foot of some ruins. He bade me sit before him, I was given coffee, my dragoman explained to him the cause of my journey, and he gave me two or three Arabs to accompany me wherever I should judge relevant.' The image gives us the bustle of the encounter: gifts are laid out, pipes smoked, coffee served *(plate 32)*. Its emphasis on the details of local costume, including that worn by the artist, serves as an implicit rebuke to Hamilton's classicising treatment of Wood and Dawkins – even as it remains within a heroising mode through the centrality of the artist, the intensity of gesture, and the ambitiously contorted horse rearing on the right.

The first photographs of Palmyra show us Volney's empty city, not Cassas's lively town; or, to put it another way, they emphasise the architectural over the picturesque. In 1864 Louis Vignes, a lieutenant in the French Navy, took some 29 views of the ruins, in which only one human figure appears – and no animals. Vignes renders the Temple of Baalshamin as an abstract essay in form, a perforated rectangular prism that teeters precariously between earth and sky and is wholly without legible scale *(plate 33)* – a contrast to Haynes's view *(plate 1)*. Closer in sensibility to Haynes's views of Palmyra are those of Félix Bonfils (1831–85), a Frenchman who established a studio in Beirut in 1867. A prolific photographer, Bonfils recorded historic monuments across the eastern Mediterranean and Middle East, and his works were eagerly acquired by tourists, becoming some of the most familiar views of the people and historic monuments of the Middle East. Although better known for his views of ancient Egypt, the Holy Land and Baalbek, Bonfils also shot more than two dozen views of

32 *Views of the ancient cities of the eastern Mediterranean by Louis-François Cassas (1756–1827) combine close attention to architectural detail with a flair for the dramatic. In this image, the propylaeum to the Temple of Bel hosts a clamorous reception for the arriving artist, who represents himself bending a knee and presenting gifts to the leader of the local community*

Palmyra between 1867 and 1876 *(following pages and plates 34, 35 and 37)*.

In 1870 the American William Stillman published his folio volume of *The Acropolis of Athens: Illustrated Picturesquely and Architecturally in Photography*. The subtitle includes a remarkable claim – that a photograph can assume both the documentary function of the architectural drawing and the artistic ambitions of the picturesque view, meant to capture a fleeting moment in the history of a site. By the second half of the nineteenth century the Acropolis had been cleared of its post-Classical accretions, including the busy town visible in eighteenth-century views of the Parthenon and Erechtheion, so Stillman's 'picturesque' related more to the momentary play of light across stone than to interactions between monuments and living beings. Haynes, who studied photography with Stillman, would find a more apt testing ground for the synthesis of the architectural and the picturesque in the still-inhabited site of Palmyra.

Haynes's photographs of Palmyra are not only more numerous than those of Vignes or Bonfils, they are also far more populated. Nearly half include at least one figure. A few also include donkeys, including the beast and rider who have wandered into the middle of the portico and the centre of Haynes's frame, apparently oblivious to the proceedings *(see plate 53)*. These latter serve as reminders of a key difference between Haynes's photographs and earlier views. In Wood's volume, the 'Arabs' delineated by the draughtsman Borra are types that conform remarkably well to Wood's descriptions. The figures in Haynes's photographs, by contrast, are individuals, little susceptible to the photographer's will.

In what may be the most remarkable of Haynes's images, a group of women do the laundry in a small stream *(plate 38)*. For all that Palmyra's allure is perennially bound up with the story of its Queen Zenobia, this is the first picture that we have of women at Palmyra, made some two centuries after the earliest travellers' accounts. It is also the first attempt to depict the life of the community without reference to the foreign visitors – unless it is the expedition's linens that are piled up on the rock in the centre.

Pictures have a way of becoming real, nowhere more so than at archaeological sites. If Haynes's approach was unobtrusive and capacious, the balance of tradition was against him. In 1930 the dwellings were cleared from the Temple of Bel, and the residents relocated. Palmyra in the late twentieth and early twenty-first centuries had been remade to meet tourists' expectations. The camels at rest in a snapshot taken by one of the authors in 2009 at the Temple of Baalshamin have been imported from the world of Hamilton or Cassas *(plate 36)*. Thus Haynes's photos of Palmyra deserve our attention not only for their early date, the extent of their coverage, or even their photographer's sensitive eye for architecture. They provide our best view of the ecology of the place, a balance between animals, people and things now fully irrecoverable.

33 *A view of the Temple of Baalshamin by Louis Vignes (1780–1862). Although Vignes learned photography from Charles Nègre, an early practitioner who initially trained as a painter, his views are mostly workmanlike. As a naval officer seconded to a scientific expedition, he continued in his career, eventually rising to the rank of vice-admiral*

34 Above and previous pages *A view by Félix Bonfils (1835–85) looking down the Great Colonnade towards the Monumental Arch, with the Temple of Bel in the distance; it is similar to Haynes's view (plate 60)*

35 *Looking down the Great Colonnade, Bonfils finds a dramatic perspective with the receding columns. Based in Beirut, he took more than two dozen photographs of Palmyra between 1867 and 1876*

36 *The Temple of Baalshamin photographed in April 2009 by Benjamin Anderson. Two camels do their best to sustain the picturesque*

37 *The Temple of Baalshamin photographed by Félix Bonfils in the 19th century. In contrast to Haynes, whose views are often inhabited by his companions or the locals, Bonfils's compositions look staged, usually with a single tiny figure set against the monumentality of the architecture*

Bonfils

38 *Local women do their washing at a spring before the rough mud walls of the village. In the background are the temenos walls of the Temple of Bel. This is the earliest known traveller's image of women at Palmyra*

THE WOLFE EXPEDITION IN PALMYRA

The ultimate goal of the Wolfe Expedition lay in Mesopotamia, not in the familiar Classical sites of the Mediterranean coasts. Palmyra lay somewhere in between; it was a fascinating detour for the expedition, but little more than that. During their days there, Ward devoted himself to the Semitic inscriptions. He instructed Sterrett to copy Greek inscriptions, although the latter grumbled that most were already known – which did not prevent him from eventually publishing ten Greek inscriptions and one Latin from the site. Haynes meanwhile photographed as much as he could. It is hard to get a sense of his movements from his photographic log, with entries marked 'Portico from east', or simply 'Colonnade', or more curiously, 'Columns of a something standing in a circle'. He began at the Marona house-tomb *(plate 40)*, presumably because it was distinctive and visible from the Temple of Baalshamin. From there he wandered to Diocletian's Camp, taking a panorama standing on top of the ruins of the *principia (plates 16 and 42)*. Rather than making a systematic survey of the site, Haynes seems to have sought out good vantage points and evocative monuments. His diary notes the number of photographs he took each day, but little more.

Ward was particularly excited as he came across the immense panel of the Palmyrene Tariff inscription – he calls it the 'octroi edict' in his travel account – which he believed to be unpublished. The local man who had showed it to him claimed no previous traveller had seen it or copied it. Accordingly, they dug it free of the sand and recorded the Aramaic and Greek texts. Both were fragmentary, but between the two Ward could recover its meaning. He even tried to make a squeeze, but the paper was stolen as they left it to dry. Haynes's one photograph of the inscription survives *(plate 43)*, alongside two views of the Tariff Court *(plates 44–45)*.

Believing he had found a great treasure, Ward was subsequently disappointed to learn from the French consul in Damascus that it had just been published. In fact, it had been published several times: by its alleged discoverer, the Russian prince S. S. Abamelek-Lazarev, as well as by H. Dessau, both in 1884, and by Melchior de Vogüé the year before. In 1901 the inscription was given as a diplomatic gift from the Ottoman Sultan to the Russian Tsar and now resides in the State Hermitage Museum in St Petersburg. Ironically, it languished two full years at the port of Odessa because of unpaid import taxes before completing its journey.

At Palmyra, the local *mudir* (governor) allowed the Wolfe team to examine and photograph a collection of twenty or thirty portrait busts, most of which had been confiscated from the tomb looters *(plates 12, 49–50)*. Ward and the others also examined the tombs in detail, although Haynes only photographed them from the exterior, occasionally including details of the funerary portraits.

Haynes seems to have been increasingly drawn back to the spine of the city, the decumanus with its picturesque colonnades, its curious Monumental Arch and its ruined temples. The villagers and donkeys that wander through his views give a sense of daily life amid the ruins.

Both Haynes and Sterrett wished to prolong their stay, but Ward was anxious to return home. 'We feel we need another day to look about and gather up the ends and fix more lastingly in the mind,' writes Haynes, as they packed to depart. He and Sterrett celebrated the end of their labours by bathing in the sulphurous Efqa Spring to the west of the Damascus Gate. Finally they visited the village that had grown up around the Temple of Bel. 'The dirty village is crowded into a small space,' Haynes wrote. 'Only one gate gives entrance but several small openings through mere holes in the castle walls. Saw a cow driven through a hole in the wall so small that she had to lower her back to crawl through. It is said to contain four or five hundred houses, but it is hard to believe there are 500 and yet it is so said.' The population may have decreased to fifty households by that time; all were removed and the population relocated to the present town several decades later to make the temple accessible to archaeology.

Looking back at Haynes's life, Palmyra stands as an appropriate landmark in his career: between his formative years in Athens and Assos, where he began his photography and had his first exposure to archaeology, and his maturity at Babylonian Nippur, where he spent the final decade of his professional life as an archaeologist and photographer. Palmyra, like Haynes himself, lay somewhere in between, fully acquainted with West and East and yet fully satisfied by neither. Today we can only imagine Haynes's response to Palmyra after months in Mesopotamia – his notebooks convey a general sense of excitement, but little more. 'An hour out we sighted the ruins of the once great city of Odenathus and Zenobia,' he writes. 'I galloped on arriving ahead of the caravan selecting quarters among the extensive and once celebrated ruins.' Still, none of his Mesopotamian photography from the Wolfe Expedition compares with the drama of his earlier Assos or Anatolian views. Palmyra, by contrast, offered a subject with which he could immediately engage, as the photographs gathered here amply testify. His diary records a final salute to the city as they departed: 'Left the once magnificent city of Zenobia's Kingdom. Left the little sun temple with not a little regret.'

39 *Looking northwards at the remains of the nymphaeum on the Great Colonnade, with the Temple of Baalshamin in the distance to the right, and the ruins of an ancient residential area to the left*

40 Above and previous pages *The house-tomb of a wealthy merchant, Julius Aurelius Marona, dated to 236, lies isolated to the north of the city. This mausoleum, built of enormous stone blocks, was the first monument to be photographed by Haynes; Sterrett and a companion stand to either side*

41 *A fragmentary sculpture of a reclining figure (on the left) and architectural ornaments, probably from the Marona house-tomb*

42 *The 'principia' at Diocletian's Camp, looking northwest into the interior of the apsidal room. This was the 'cella', or inner chamber, of the temple that housed the standards of the Roman legion, built c. 293–303*

43 *The Palmyrene Tariff, erected in the year AD137. The bilingual inscription in Greek and Aramaic is a unique source for the history of the Roman economy. It is now displayed in the Hermitage Museum, St Petersburg*

44 *The entrance to the Tariff Court, where the famed inscription was discovered. Originally a grand triple entrance, the southern entrance was partially dismantled when the medieval fortification wall was built*

45 *The central entrance to the Tariff Court, looking south, with the colonnade of a cross street in the distance*

FUNERARY MONUMENTS

46 *The Tower Tomb of Elahbel (no. 13) and his three brothers, built in AD 103, is the largest of the Palmyrene tower tombs. In the arch above the door is a couch which originally supported a figure of the deceased. Haynes composed the photograph to include tower tombs in the middle and far distance*

47 *The imposing Tomb of Iamblichus (no. 51), dated to the year AD83, was the first tower to be built of dressed stone, rising above a stepped base, with a moulded profile at its summit and a detailed pediment above its portal. The brackets halfway up supported figures of winged victories, which once framed a relief of a funerary banquet*

48 *Tower Tomb 71 is missing its dedicatory inscription but must date from the middle of the first century AD. An internal staircase connected the various levels*

49 *Three funerary portraits from the collection of the 'mudir'. A mother gestures towards the child held at her breast; a clean-shaven man is dressed in Roman fashion; a woman wears a typical Palmyrene headdress but clutches her veil in a Roman gesture of modesty*

50 *Three funerary portraits from the same collection. A woman holds up her palm, warding off evil with an apotropaic gesture; a priest with a conical hat holds a branch and gestures with his hands; another priest, lavishly garbed with an ornamental collar and brooch, holds vessels for libations*

51 *A travelling companion poses at the entrance of a collapsed tower tomb constructed of impressively large stone blocks*

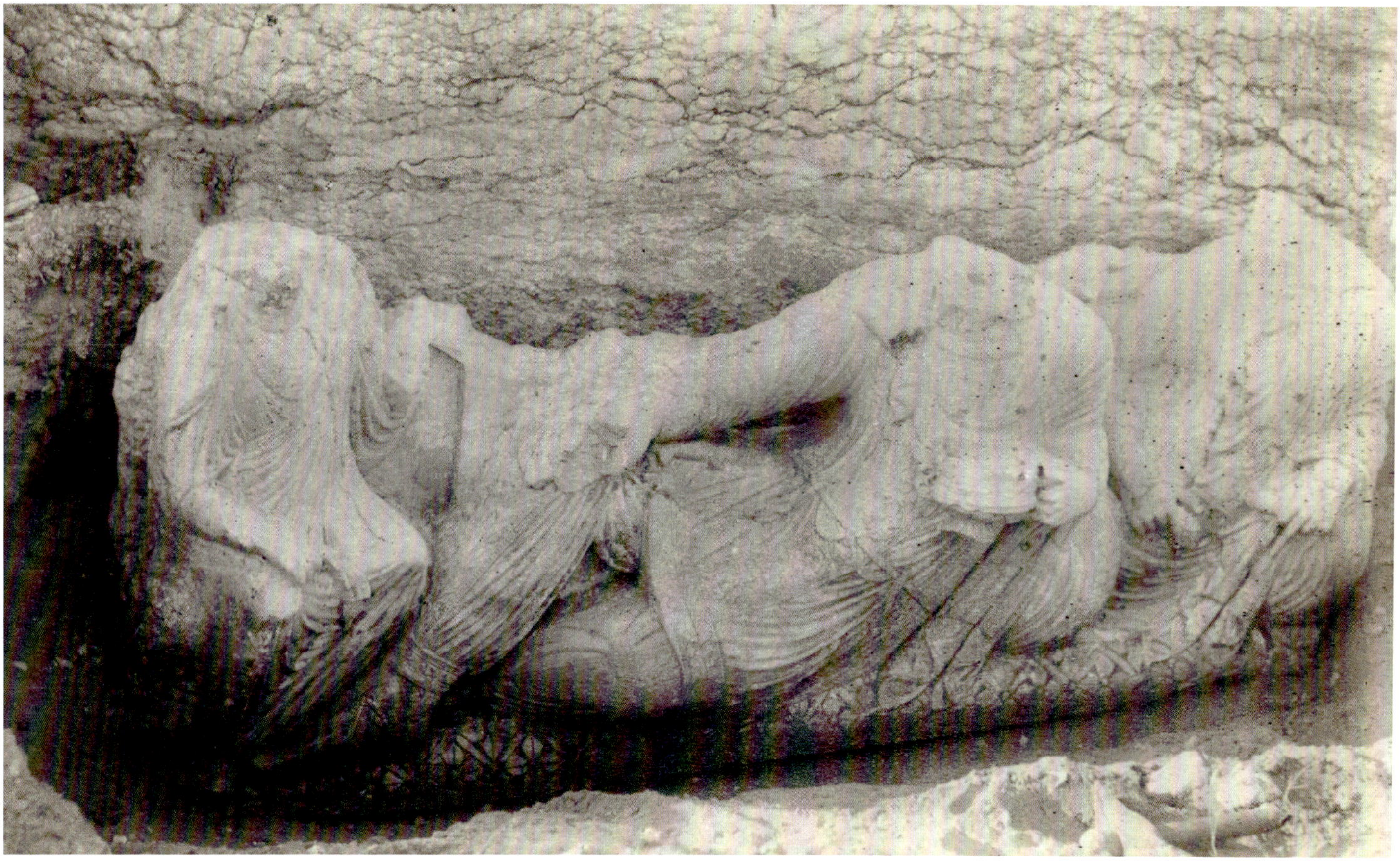

52 *A partially excavated headless funerary group depicts two figures reclining on a lavishly embroidered couch, with a servant sitting to one side*

THE GREAT COLONNADE

53 ABOVE AND PREVIOUS PAGES *The Great Colonnade, Palmyra's main street, stretches from west to east for more than a kilometre – almost three-quarters of a mile – connecting the Temple of Bel to the Camp of Diocletian. This section is close to the entrance to the Baths of Diocletian. The remains of the Theatre, still partially buried in Haynes's day, are on the left in the middle distance*

54 *One of the landmarks of Palmyra, the Monumental Arch was constructed during the reign of Septimius Severus (AD 193–211) at the height of the city's prosperity. Technically not a triumphal arch, it was decorative in purpose: it is built across the Great Colonnade, its wedge-shaped plan subtly resolving the change of axis as the street turns south to meet the Temple of Bel – from which the photograph was taken*

55 *The Monumental Arch seen from the area of the Temple of Nabu, screened by the Great Colonnade*

56 *Columns on the street leading to the Damascus Gate are equipped with double brackets, while those of the Great Colonnade in the distance have single brackets, all intended for statues honouring the merchants and traders of Palmyra on whom the prosperity of the city rested*

57 *A fallen column drum carved from a single block of stone, with brackets on two sides to support honorific statues*

58 *Looking north across the porticoes of the Great Colonnade between the oval forum and the nymphaeum, with the Temple of Baalshamin in the distance*

59 *The columns of the Great Colonnade frame views of the distant tower tombs at Umm al-Belqis and on the hills beyond*

60 *The Monumental Arch looking southeast, with the Temple of Bel in the distance and a section of the Great Colonnade on the right. The columns preserve their brackets, which once supported statues of local worthies who funded the construction of the porticoes. This is a similar view to the one captured earlier by Bonfils (plate 34)*

61 *A view towards the now-destroyed Monumental Arch through the peristyle of the Baths of Diocletian*

62 *The Monumental Arch seen from the south. The medieval castle rises in the distance above the Great Colonnade, while the small arch on the right frames a view to the Temple of Baalshamin*

63 *The Monumental Arch seen from the northwest, with the Temple of Bel in the distance. To the right, a section of the Great Colonnade forms part of the enclosure of the Temple of Nabu, god of wisdom (see plate 55)*

64 *Seen from the south, the Monumental Arch appears as a ruin amid the ruins, the logic of its wedge-shaped plan now difficult to understand*

65 *The architraves and capitals of the Great Colonnade appear above the mound in the foreground, which conceals the remains of the second-century Roman Theatre, still buried in Haynes's day. Once it had been excavated and restored in the 1950s, the theatre became one of the city's most prominent monuments*

66 *A break in a colonnaded cross street frames a view of the medieval castle of Qalaat Shirkuh. The wall immediately behind the colonnade belongs to the Tariff Court*

67 Above and previous pages *Haynes records: 'Our men at table at our quarters by the little sun temple [Temple of Baalshamin]. Our four men, two zaptiyehs [gendarmes] from Ed Deir [Deir ez-Zor], our kourdish katirgee [muleteer] & servant at Tedmor. Also another serving man behind them.'*

68 *Sterrett, after he had recovered from the serious illness that had stranded him in Baghdad, posing amid the ruins of Palmyra, framed by doorposts inscribed with winged victories*

69 The remains of a peristyle house in the northern part of the city. Because the walls of the house were constructed of brick, only the stone columns and architrave of the peristyle remain standing. Sterrett (seated) and Noorian pose with the Temple of Bel in the distance

70 *All that remains of an atrium house are the four columns that once framed the impluvium, the sunken pool in the centre of the atrium that received rainwater from an opening in the roof. Haynes wrongly identified the house as a mausoleum. The servants Mustapher and Artin and the Kurdish guard Halil sit inside the atrium. The two right-hand columns frame the funerary temple*

71 *The funerary temple at the western end of the decumanus forms a visual terminus for the grand colonnaded street. Dating from the early third century AD, and the only tomb inside the city, it is sometimes associated with the family of Odenathus and Zenobia. Only this temple-like façade was standing at the time of Haynes's visit*

72 *Ruins envelop the standing façade of the funerary temple. These unaccountably fascinated Ward, who requested photographs. Haynes's journal lists this view dismissively as 'Dr. Ward's heap of rubbish'. One of their travelling companions poses at the top of the heap*

73 *More of 'Dr. Ward's heap of rubbish' to the east of the funerary temple*

74 *Another evocative area of collapse near the Great Colonnade*

75 Above and previous pages *A view from the modern cemetery near the Temple of Bel, looking north towards the Monumental Arch and the Great Colonnade, with Qalaat Shirkuh in the distance. Inscribed ancient stone blocks have been reused as pillars in the more recent tombs*

THE TEMPLE OF BEL

76 *The enormous temenos of the Temple of Bel seen from the north. Measuring 205 by 210 metres overall, the enclosure wall was added in the second and third centuries. The temple precinct was reinforced and converted into a fortress in the Middle Ages*

77 *A rebuilt wall of the temenos of the Temple of Bel, the columns of its double portico rising behind it, while the ashlar blocks of its original construction lie tumbled in the foreground*

78 *The Temple of Bel, with the remains of the more recent Arab village of Tadmur in the foreground. The temple and its enormous precinct date from the first and second centuries. By the twelfth century, the 'cella' had been converted to a mosque, and a village developed around it – the latter dismantled by the French administration in 1930. The temple was destroyed in 2015*

79 Above and inside back cover *The monumental propylaeum of the Temple of Bel was converted into a fortified entrance in the twelfth century. The area between the second-century 'antae', or pilasters, was walled in, leaving only a small entrance guarded by the machicolations above*

80 *The open spaces within the temenos of Bel are filled with houses*

81 *The eastern façade of the great Temple of Bel, with the remains of the old village of Tadmur in the foreground. The 'cella' of the temple served as the village mosque until the 1920s*

82 *The monumental western entrance to the Temple of Bel*

83 *At the Temple of Bel, the plain columns of the portico of the temenos, on the left, contrast with the fluted columns of the temple itself behind. The enclosure in between is filled with the rough houses of the Arab village*

84 *The columns of the portico rise above the mud and rubble houses within the temenos of the Temple of Bel. With the jumble of residences and the 'cella' used as a mosque, Haynes and his companions had limited access to the site*

QALAAT SHIRKUH

85 *Qalaat Shirkuh seen from the south, with a ruined tower tomb in the foreground. The castle was long attributed to the seventeenth-century emir Fakhr al-Din ibn Maan, but its origins are probably earlier – twelfth or thirteenth century – and contemporary with the fortification of the Temple of Bel*

THE AUTHORS

Benjamin Anderson is an Assistant Professor in the History of Art Department at Cornell University. His research engages with the visual and material cultures of the Eastern Mediterranean and adjacent landmasses, with a focus on late antique and Byzantine art and architecture. His forthcoming book *Cosmos and Community in Early Medieval Art* will be published by Yale University Press.

Robert G. Ousterhout, Professor in the History of Art Department at the University of Pennsylvania, has long been involved in the analysis and documentation of the vanishing cultural heritage of the Eastern Mediterranean. He is the author of *John Henry Haynes: A Photographer and Archaeologist in the Ottoman Empire 1881–1900* (Caique Publishing, 2011, revised edition 2016). His forthcoming book *Visualizing Community: Art, Material Culture, and Settlement in Byzantine Cappadocia* will be published by Dumbarton Oaks Press.

ACKNOWLEDGEMENTS

While the Archaeological Institute of America no longer has a photographic archive, it preserves the substantial correspondence from Haynes to its President, Charles Eliot Norton, at their Boston office. Surviving photographs from Haynes's personal collection are divided between the archives of the University of Pennsylvania Museum of Archaeology and Anthropology and the Documentation Center of the Aga Khan Program for Islamic Architecture at the Fine Arts Library, Harvard University – the latter purchased on eBay from Haynes's descendants. His travel diaries and letters are similarly divided. The photographs from the Cornell University Library were collected by J.R. Sitlington Sterrett and are held in the Division of Rare and Manuscript Collections (Archives #4776). Production of the digital files used for this volume was funded by the DCAPS Grant Program for Digital Collections in Arts and Sciences. We wish especially to thank Rhea Garen, Hannah Marshall, Danielle Mericle and Eisha Neely at the Cornell University Library for their kind assistance. We are grateful to Alessandro Pezzati and Eric Schnittke at the Archives of the University of Pennsylvania Museum and to Andras Riedlmayer and Joanne Bloom at Harvard for making additional photographs available to us.

BIBLIOGRAPHY

PALMYRA

As'ad, Khaled and Jean-Baptiste Yon, *Inscriptions de Palmyre* (Paris, 2001)

Bosworth, Charles E.
'Tadmur', *Encyclopedia of Islam, Second Edition*

Browning, Iain, *Palmyra* (London, 1979)

Butcher, Kevin
Roman Syria and the Near East (Los Angeles, 2003)

Genequand, Denis, 'An Early Islamic Mosque in Palmyra, *Levant* 40 (2008), 3–15

Halifax, William, 'A Relation of a Voyage from Aleppo to Palmyra in Syria', *Philosophical Transactions* 19, no. 217 (1695): 83–110

Goodyear, Aaron and Timothy Lanoy, 'An Extract of the Journals of Two Several Voyages of the English Merchants of the Factory of Aleppo, to Tadmor, Anciently Call'd Palmyra', *Philosophical Transactions* 19, no. 218 (1695): 129–160

Majcherek, Grzegorz
'Excavating the Basilicas', *Studia Palmyreskie* 12 (2013): 251–268

Matthews, J. F.
'The Tax Law of Palmyra: Evidence for Economic History in a City of the Roman East', *Journal of Roman Studies* 74 (1984): 157–180

Millar, Fergus
The Roman Near East: 31 BC – AD 337 (Cambridge, MA, 1993)

Sauvaget, Jean, 'Inscriptions arabes du Temple de Bêl à Palmyre', *Syria* 12 (1931): 143–153

Schmidt-Colinet, Andreas, ed.
Palmyra: Kulturbegegnung im Grenzbereich (Mainz am Rhein, 2005)

Shifman, Ilya Sholeimovich, *The Palmyrene Tax Tariff* (Oxford, 2014)

Smith, Andrew M.
Roman Palmyra: Identity, Community, and State Formation (Oxford, 2013)

Stoneman, Richard
Palmyra and Its Empire: Zenobia's Revolt against Rome (Ann Arbor, 1992)

Wood, Robert
The Ruins of Palmyra, Otherwise Tedmor, in the Desart (London, 1753)

HAYNES AND THE WOLFE EXPEDITION

Geere, H. Valentine
By Nile and Euphrates: A Record of Discovery and Adventure (London, 1904)

Haynes, John Henry
Unpublished travel diaries, 1884–85, University of Pennsylvania Museum Archives

Hilprecht, Herman V.
Explorations in Bible Lands during the 19th Century (Philadelphia, 1903)

Holod, Renata, and Rober G. Ousterhout, eds.
Osman Hamdi Bey & the Americans: archaeology, diplomacy, art (Istanbul 2011)

Kuklick, Bruce
Puritans in Babylon: The Ancient Near East and American Intellectual Life, 1800–1930 (Princeton, 1996)

Lyons, Claire L., John K. Papadopoulos, Lindsey S. Stewart, and Andrew Szegedy-Mascak
Antiquity & Photography: Early Views of Ancient Mediterranean Sites (Los Angeles, 2006)

Ousterhout, Robert G.
John Henry Haynes: A Photographer and Archaeologist in the Ottoman Empire, 1881–1900 (Istanbul and Edinburgh, 2011)

Peters, John P.
Nippur or Explorations and Adventures on the Euphrates 2 vols. (New York, 1897, 1904)

Sterrett, John Robert Sitlington
Preliminary Report on an Epigraphical Journey Made in Asia Minor during the Summer of 1884 (Boston, 1885)
—— *The Wolfe Expedition to Asia Minor* (Boston, 1888)

Ward, William Hayes
Report on the Wolfe Expedition to Babylonia 1884–85 (Boston, 1886)

PICTURE CREDITS

BENJAMIN ANDERSON
38 (schematic plan, page 35)

CORNELL UNIVERSITY LIBRARY The Carl A. Kroch Library
1, 6, 12, 13 (and cover), 14, 15, 16, 17, 18, 19, 20, 21, 22, 23, 24, 25, 27, 28, 31, 37, 38, 39, 40, 41, 42, 43, 44, 45, 47, 48, 49, 50, 51, 52, 53, 54, 55, 56, 57, 59, 60, 61, 62, 63, 64, 65, 66, 67, 69, 70, 71, 72, 73, 74, 75, 76, 77, 78, 79, 80, 81, 82, 83, 84, 85

GETTY RESEARCH INSTITUTE
33

HAK ARCHIVES / HARVARD UNIVERSITY
Documentation Center of the Aga Khan Program for Islamic Architecture, courtesy of Special Collections, Fine Arts Library
4, 9

HARVARD ART MUSEUMS / FOGG MUSEUM
Gift of Belinda L. Randall from the collection of John Witt Randall, R2595. Photo: Imaging Department © President and Fellows of Harvard College
30

UNIVERSITÄTSBIBLIOTHEK HEIDELBERG
29, 32

UPM ARCHIVES
University of Pennsylvania Museum of Archaeology and Anthropology, Philadelphia, PA, Archives
2, 3, 5, 7, 8, 10, 26, 34, 35, 36, 46, 58, 68

Wikimedia Commons / Classical Numismatic Group, Inc.
11

A CORNUCOPIA BOOK
First published in 2016 by Caique Publishing Ltd,
1 Rutland Court, Edinburgh EH3 8EY

ISBN 978-0-9565948-7-7

PROJECT EDITORS John Scott, Berrin Torolsan
TEXT EDITORS Susana Raby, Hilary Stafford-Clark, Tony Barrell

DESIGN Clive Crook and Debi Angel

SPECIAL IMAGING Orhan Gündüz

Printed and bound in Turkey
Ofset Yapımevi, Istanbul
www.ofset.com

CORNUCOPIA BOOKS
PO Box 13311, Hawick TD9 7YF
www.cornucopia.net